KU-455-390

# SO MANY QUESTIONS about...
# BUILDINGS

## Sally Spray and Mark Ruffle

S00000913006

First published in Great Britain in 2021 by Wayland
© Hodder and Stoughton Limited, 2021

All rights reserved.

HB ISBN: 978 1 5263 1764 3
PB ISBN: 978 1 5263 1765 0

Editor: Paul Rockett
Design and illustration: Mark Ruffle
www.rufflebrothers.com

Printed in Dubai

Wayland
An imprint of Hodder Children's Group
Part of Hodder & Stoughton
Carmelite House
50 Victoria Embankment
London EC4Y 0DZ

An Hachette UK Company
www.hachette.co.uk
www.hachettechildrens.co.uk

The website addresses (URLs) included in this book were valid at
the time of going to press. However, it is possible that contents or
addresses may have changed since the publication of this book.
No responsibility for any such changes can be accepted by either
the author or the Publisher.

| DUDLEY LIBRARIES | |
| --- | --- |
| S00000913006 | |
| Askews & Holts | 12-Oct-2022 |
| C720 | £8.99 |
| 2SLS | |

# Have you ever thought about buildings?
# Think of all the questions you could ask ...

**Do you know about buildings?
I have lots of questions for you.**

Oh yes, buildings
are my speciality!

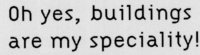

# Why do we need buildings?

We need buildings for all sorts of things. People can live in them and stay dry and feel safe. Some are specially built for work and school, and for fun things like watching films and playing sport. You can store things in them, such as grain or an aircraft, and there are even glass buildings that help plants to grow inside.

Most buildings have a roof that protects those inside from the sun, wind and rain.

**Think about ...** the buildings that you know.

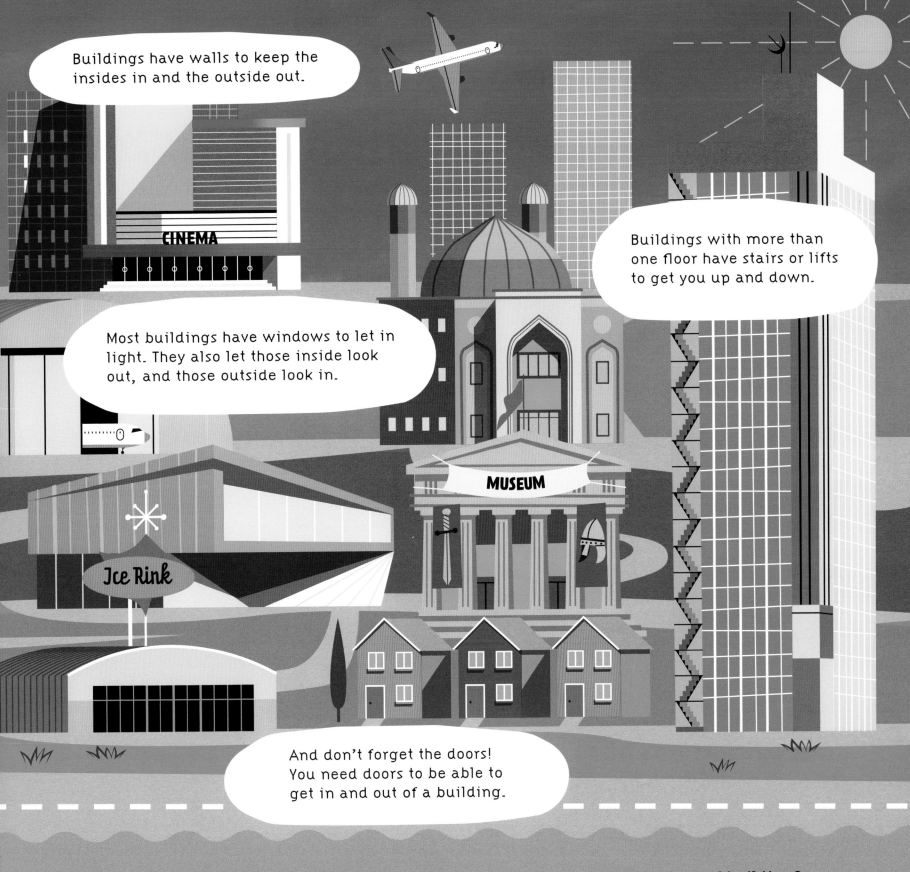

What features are important for buildings? What features would you add to the building you live in?

What is your favourite type of building? How are supermarket buildings different from school buildings?

# What were the first buildings?

We don't really know when the first buildings were constructed, but we do know that building materials and tools were in use about 12,000 years ago. There are ancient ruins around the world that help us learn what early people built and how they lived. Here are some examples ...

About 20,000 years ago, people living in the area of modern Ukraine built what might be the first homes. They used mammoth bones and skins.

The city of **Çatalhöyük** in Turkey existed between 7100 BCE–5700 BCE. Here, around 7,000 people lived in back-to-back mud-brick houses. The buildings did not have doors. Instead people entered their homes through a hatch on the roof.

**Think about ...** old buildings in your local area.

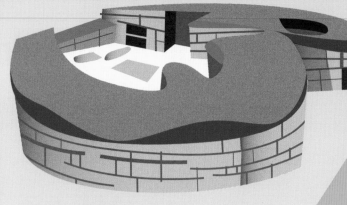

**Caral-Supe** is the most ancient city of the Americas, near the coast of Peru. It was built around 2600 BCE, and today you can see the remains of stone houses, temples, an amphitheatre and even pyramids.

Around the Alps, on 111 different sites, archaeologists have found the remains of **pile dwellings**. Built near rivers, and dating from between 5000 BCE–500 BCE, people built these wooden houses using tools made of bone, stone and iron.

**Skara Brae** in Orkney, Scotland, is a settlement of stone houses occupied about 5,000 years ago. The linked homes had roofs that were probably made from turf, seaweed and woven straw. Each home had stone beds, a hearth and shelves.

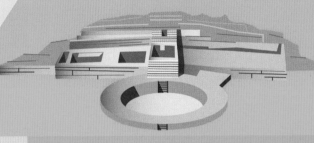

The **Nanchan Temple**, built in 782, is the oldest wooden building standing in China today. It's unusual for wooden buildings to have survived for so long without getting damaged by fire, earthquakes, damp or eaten by woodworm!

The **Ziggurat of Ur**, in present-day Iraq, is a temple built around 2100 BCE to honour Nanna, the moon god. It's a pyramid structure, built to be close to the sky. Staircases lead to terraces, on which the temple once stood.

The **Colosseum** is an ancient entertainment venue in Rome, Italy. Built between 70 and 80 CE, this open-air amphitheatre could hold over 50,000 people who came to see gladiator fights and other shows.

What is the oldest building you know?
How is it different to modern buildings?

Which of its features do you like most?
How were old buildings kept warm or cool?

# What are the most famous buildings in the world?

There are many famous buildings all over the world. They may be well-known because they are very tall, very old, breathtakingly beautiful, or weird and wonderful. Some have become symbols of their cities.

The **Empire State Building**, New York, USA is supported by a strong steel skeleton, secured in 17-m-deep concrete foundations.

The **Willis Tower**, Chicago, USA can sway up to 90-cm in windy weather.

**Tikal**, Guatemala had about 4,000 buildings and was the centre of the Mayan Empire.

**Machu Picchu**, Peru sits on top of a mountain. It's built from tightly packed stones and no mortar.

The **Niterói Contemporary Art Museum**, Brazil looks like a UFO that has landed by the sea. It was completed in 1996.

**Think about ...** the famous buildings that you know.

**Hagia Sophia**, Istanbul, Turkey has a large 32-m diameter dome, and four minarets.

**St Basil's Cathedral**, Moscow, Russia was built in 1561 by the scary sounding Ivan the Terrible.

The **Taj Mahal**, Agra, India was built from marble and stone delivered by 1,000 elephants.

In **Shanghai**, China, there's a trio of sky-tickling skyscrapers:

The **Shanghai Tower** is 632 m tall and has a twisting, aerodynamic shape.

**Shanghai World Financial Centre** is 492 m tall. It has an opening allowing wind to rush through.

The **Jin Mao Tower** is 348 m tall. The design is based on traditional Chinese pagodas.

Shanghai Tower

Shanghai World Financial Centre

Jin Mao Tower

The **Fjordenhus**, Denmark uses glazed bricks to reflect light from the Vejle fjord where it sits.

The **Parthenon**, Greece has 46 outer columns and 19 inner columns holding up the roof.

The **Petronas Towers**, Kuala Lumpur, Malaysia are separate buildings joined at the 42nd floor by a sky-bridge.

The **Great Mosque of Djenné**, Mali is built of mud bricks. It sits on a platform to protect it from floods.

The **Bosjes Farm Chapel**, South Africa has glass walls and a curvy, undulating roof.

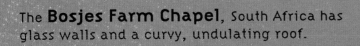

The **Pyramids of Giza** were built 4,500 years ago as tombs for Pharaohs. There are about 138 pyramids in Egypt.

The **Sydney Opera House**, Australia is a space for music, dance and theatre. The 14 roofs were inspired by segments of oranges.

Why do you think buildings become famous?
Would you like to live in a famous building?
What would you like about it?

Find out about other famous buildings.
Where in the world are they?

# What are buildings made of?

Buildings are made using natural materials like wood and stone and man-made materials like bricks and metal. Let's look more closely at some of the most common construction materials ...

**Concrete** is a strong material. It starts life as a liquid and can be poured into different moulds and then sets like rock. It can be made even stronger by reinforcing it with metal wires or bars.

**Bricks** come in lots of shapes, sizes and colours. They're made from sand and clay and are baked until hard. They last for a long time and are easy to build with – if you practise! The bricks are held together with mortar.

**Stone** is an ancient building material. It's dug from the ground and cut into blocks for bricks or slabs.

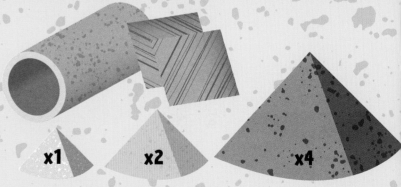

**x1**  **x2**  **x4**

**Concrete recipe:** Mix one part cement, two parts sand and four parts aggregate (small stones and gravel). Add water and leave to set!

**Think about ...** why builders need to use dfferent building materials.

Outside it's bumpy and lumpy, inside it's smooth with swirly, grain patterns.

**Wood** has been used as a building material for thousands of years. Cut trees are sliced into planks and sanded down. To protect the wood from weather and insects it is often treated with special chemicals.

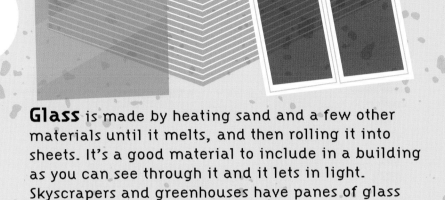

**Glass** is made by heating sand and a few other materials until it melts, and then rolling it into sheets. It's a good material to include in a building as you can see through it and it lets in light. Skyscrapers and greenhouses have panes of glass as walls.

**Mortar** is used to stick bricks together. It's made from cement, sand and water.

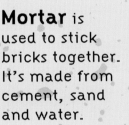

**Slate** is a natural grey stone that breaks into thin sheets and makes wonderfully, waterproof roof tiles.

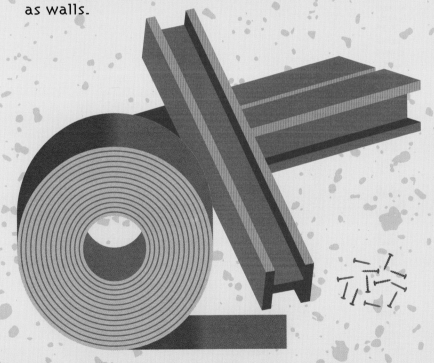

**Steel** is strong and long lasting. It can be used for the frames of buildings, as well as beams, sheets, nails and screws. It is made from a mix of iron and carbon which are heated together, shaped and cooled.

What tools do builders need to use to build with these materials?
Would you prefer to live in a house made of steel or a house made of wood?
Which of these building materials would you use to built your dream home?

# Why don't tall buildings fall over?

It has the fastest lifts in the world – 57 of them. They can whizz you from the ground to the top floor in one minute!

If you could walk up the side, it would take 15 minutes to walk the entire length.

Let's look at the **Burj Khalifa**, built in Dubai, to understand how tall buildings stay upright. It is a super tall skyscraper at 828 m high, it has 200 storeys – and it is a bit wobbly!

**Think about ...** why people build tall buildings.

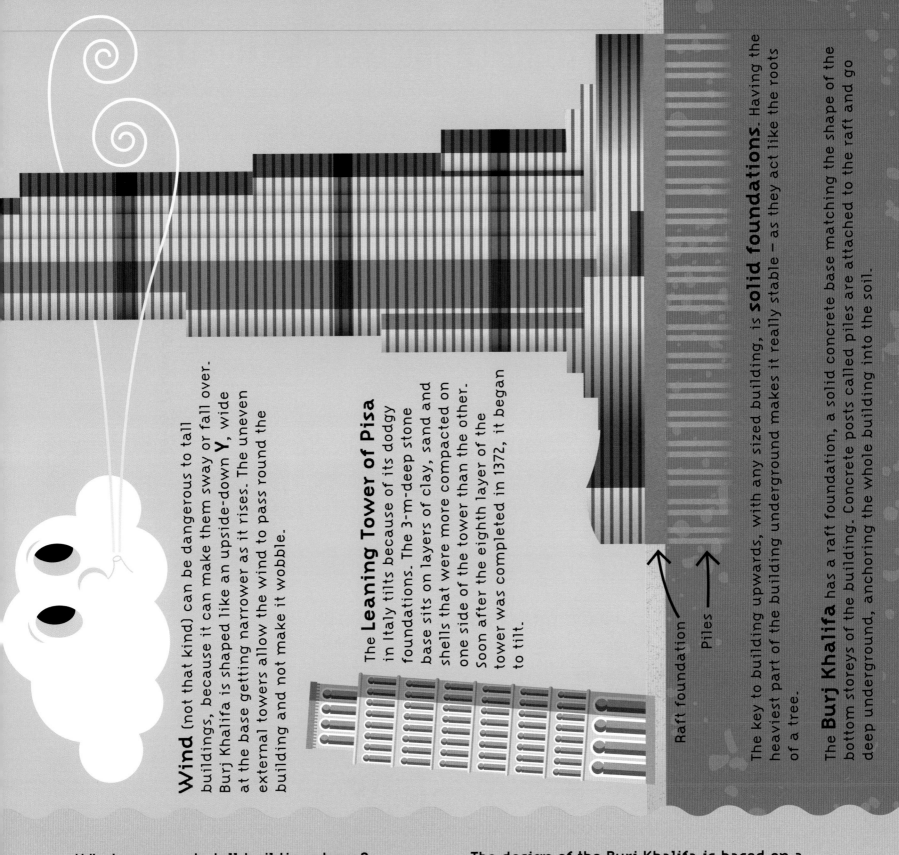

**Wind** (not that kind) can be dangerous to tall buildings, because it can make them sway or fall over. Burj Khalifa is shaped like an upside-down **Y**, wide at the base getting narrower as it rises. The uneven external towers allow the wind to pass round the building and not make it wobble.

### The **Leaning Tower of Pisa**

in Italy tilts because of its dodgy foundations. The 3-m-deep stone base sits on layers of clay, sand and shells that were more compacted on one side of the tower than the other. Soon after the eighth layer of the tower was completed in 1372, it began to tilt.

Raft foundation

Piles

The key to building upwards, with any sized building, is **solid foundations.** Having the heaviest part of the building underground makes it really stable – as they act like the roots of a tree.

The **Burj Khalifa** has a raft foundation, a solid concrete base matching the shape of the building. Concrete posts called piles are attached to the raft and go deep underground, anchoring the whole building into the soil.

What purpose do tall buildings have?
Would you like to live at the top?
Would you feel safe?

The design of the Burj Khalifa is based on a flower. What other things can you find that have designs inspired by nature?

# Are there buildings in extreme climates?

There are buildings in really extreme places. In Antarctica, one of the coldest places in the world, there are 70 permanent research buildings. This one, the **Amundsen-Scott South Pole Station,** can house between 50-150 scientists. It sits on adjustable stilts and the lower wall slopes upwards. This helps wind to flow under it at speed, clearing away any deep snow that builds up.

**Igloos** are temporary shelters made in the Arctic Circle. Carved blocks of ice are placed in a spiral to form a dome, with a tunnel to get in. A bank of snow around the base insulates the igloo, keeping it warmer inside.

**Think about ...** what it's like to live in extreme climates.

At the other extreme, these buildings can be found in hot, dry deserts.

The **Through Gardens House**, in Iran, is a modern house, built using traditional techniques which make desert living bearable. The walls are insulated against hot days and cold nights. The walls are covered in adobe, a mixture of straw and dung, and holes in the garden wall let cooling breezes in.

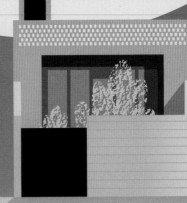

One of the strangest desert buildings is in Utah, USA. The **Mars Desert Research Station** is a series of pods to test out what it would be like to live on Mars. Volunteers live and work in the seven pods for a few weeks at a time. If they go outside, they have to wear spacesuits and communicate using radios.

Any more questions?

Yes, loads!

Turn the page then, and let's get going!

**Nomadic people** in the Sahara desert carry their tent homes with them, and build them where their animals stop to graze. The tents are supported by wooden poles and draped in fabric or animal hides. This helps protect people from the extremes of heat and cold.

Which of these buildings would you like to visit? Why? Draw a building for a cold climate. How will the design keep people warm inside?

How do animals shelter in these climates? What can we learn from them?

15

# Are there buildings underwater, in the trees and underground?

People have built buildings in all sorts of odd places. It's fun to test what is possible, live where no one else does, have a spectacular view of nature, or build something that you wouldn't find anywhere else in the world.

In Norway the world's largest underwater restaurant, **Under**, looks like it's tipped into the sea, giving diners a sea view as they tuck into their seafood dinners.

To keep the water out, the 1-m-wide walls are constructed from concrete.

The outside is textured to encourage barnacles and shellfish to make their home there.

The enormous windows have glass that is 25 cm thick.

**Think about** ... which of these buildings you would like to visit.

This amazing treehouse in Sweden is really hard to see. It's made from aluminium and completely covered in mirrored glass, which reflects the forest surroundings. The interior walls are covered in wood, so it is like being inside a tree.

Shhh! It's very quiet if you live underground.

How do you fancy an underground house? They're environmentally friendly, insulated by the surrounding soil and save up to 80 per cent of heating costs. They take up less space, fitting into the natural environment, and are resistant to high winds, earthquakes and fire.

Light shafts bring in light and air.

This is definitely my favourite – what a sensible place to build a house!

Which unusual location would you build in?
What would you need to think about?
Would it be harder to build underwater or up a tree?

What materials would you use?
Where would you feel most safe?
Where would be most fun?

# What shapes can buildings be?

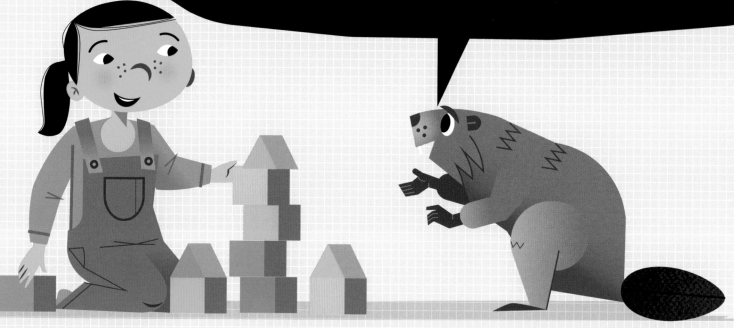

Buildings come in all shapes and sizes – straightforward straight shapes and curvy, bendy, twisty shapes. The shapes used can make a building look amazing, but also make it structurally safe and strong. Let's see some shapes in action.

**Cube Tube**, in Jinhua, China, is a **cube-shaped** office building. Each floor has lots of square windows making the insides light and bright.

The entrance to the **Louvre**, Paris is a glass and metal **pyramid** with four triangular faces or sides. It acts as a giant window, letting light into the underground atrium of the art gallery.

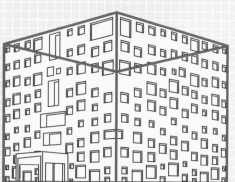

**Think about** ... how to construct buildings with these shapes.

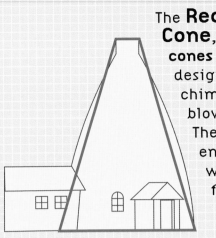

The **Red House Glass Cone**, Wordsley, UK. These **cones** were specially designed to be like a huge chimney for the glass-blowing factory inside. The ground floor is large enough for people to work, and the shape funnels heat from the furnaces up and out of the top.

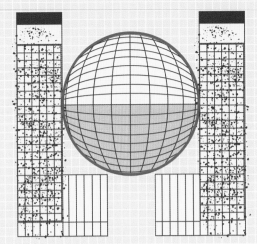

The **Nagoya City Science Museum**, Nagoya, Japan is a **spherical** building joined to two cuboids. The sphere is used as a planetarium where the rounded walls are perfect for projecting films of the starry night sky.

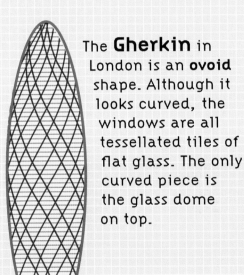

The **Gherkin** in London is an **ovoid** shape. Although it looks curved, the windows are all tessellated tiles of flat glass. The only curved piece is the glass dome on top.

The **National Centre for the Performing Arts**, Beijing, China is known as the Giant Egg. It is really an **ellipsoid**. It's surrounded by water and the reflection makes the whole thing look like an egg.

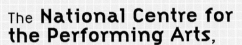

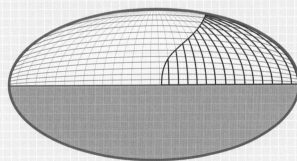

The **F&F Tower**, Panama, is a **spiral-shaped** building that soars 243 m above the ground. It's officially the tightest twist design in the world.

**Geodesic domes** have frames made from tessellated **triangles**, **squares** or **hexagons** that create their rounded shape. This structure distributes the weight of the building throughout the frame. The **Eden Project's Biomes** in Cornwall, UK, are covered in plastic. They're inspired by soap bubbles, and fit perfectly in the uneven landscape.

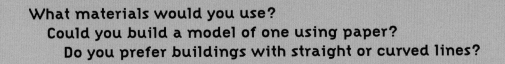

What materials would you use?
Could you build a model of one using paper?
Do you prefer buildings with straight or curved lines?

What shape building would you design?
Does the shape make it look more interesting, scary or important?

# How do we make buildings environmentally friendly?

Builders and engineers are looking for ways to make buildings more energy efficient and less damaging to the environment, by planning and thinking about their materials. The wellbeing of the people and how spaces form communities is also important to consider.

Insulation

**Natural light** is good for people. Windows can also add solar heat from the sun, warming interiors naturally.

**Insulation** keeps heat in and cold out, or the other way round, depending on where you live. Spaces in the walls and roof, called cavities, can be filled with insulating material. Insulation can also keep interiors quiet.

Buildings should be **airtight**, to keep heat in. All the spaces around the windows, doors and roof should be sealed, with no draughty gaps. But, buildings also need to be **ventilated**, allowing air to flow through windows and vents, to cool them and stop damp.

**Rainwater harvesting system**

**Think about** ... the materials you would use to design a new building.

## Green structural materials

Building with materials that are reclaimed, reused and sustainable is better for the environment and can last for a long, long time.

## Building frames

These structures can be made out of

recycled steel from cars,

compressed bamboo, which grows quickly and is stronger than wood, brick or concrete.

## Insulation

Walls can be insulated with

sheep's wool

and straw.

**Roof spaces** can be used to improve a building. Inside, they should be well insulated. Outside, they could be used as a garden.

Solar panel

## Walls

These can be made from straw bales,

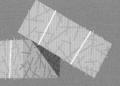

**Building materials** can be used which have good thermal mass. That is the material's ability to absorb, store and release heat.

rammed soil packed into frames or

Ground source heat pump

mycelium fungi grown through straw and air dried into bricks.

Buildings can be **self-sufficient**, collecting heat and light from renewable technologies, like solar panels, wind turbines, ground or air-source heat pumps, and water from rainwater harvesting.

How could you make your building energy efficient? Which green building materials could you use to build your structure?

How else could you reduce its impact on the local environment?

21

# Who designs buildings?

Architects design buildings. An Architect needs lots of different skills: great imagination, the skills to know what can be built, knowledge of how much things might cost, and good communication to pass on their ideas.

Here are some exciting buildings and the architects behind them.

**Zaha Hadid** (1950-2016) designed lots of curves into her buildings, like this one, the **Heydar Aliyev Centre**, Baku, Azerbaijan (2012). it was designed to flow beautifully and stand out from the buildings around it.

**Think about ...** what it takes to be an architect.

**David Adjaye's** (1966-) designs are famous for their beauty and for working well as homes or public spaces.

The **Moscow School of Management**, Skolkovo, Russia (2011) features four supported cuboid buildings, on a circular base.

**Antoni Gaudí** (1852-1926) designed buildings in his home city, Barcelona, Spain. His fantastical designs are decorated with colourful mosaics. The most famous is the **Sagrada Familia** church, which has been in construction since 1882, and is due to be completed in 2026. Gaudi is buried there, in perhaps his greatest creation.

**Richard Rogers** (1933-) and **Renzo Piano** (1937-) worked together on the **Centre Pompidou**, Paris, France (1971-77). It's exciting to look at because the stairways, pipes and wires are all on the outside of the building, leaving the exhibition spaces inside as large as they can be.

**Shigeru Ban's** (1957-) buildings are made of paper and cardboard. He uses paper coated in waterproof paint, and boxes of sand for foundations. They have been used to provide shelter for refugees from war and earthquakes. This is the **Paper Log House**, Kobe, Japan (1995).

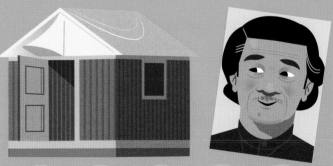

Could you design a brilliant building? What would it be for? What skills would you need?

What shapes and materials would you use? What would make it stand out from other buildings?

# Can animals build?

Of course! **Beavers** build enormous dams to redirect river water into ponds where we live. We fell trees and strip branches for the dam with our giant front teeth. Our dens are built in the dam and you have to dive down to get inside them. The dens have two chambers, one for drying off and one where we sleep.

## Baya weaver birds

weave nests from grass and leaf strips. They secure the nest to a branch with a loop of grass, then weave a spherical space with a tube-shaped entrance. It keeps the chicks cosy and safe.

**Wasps** build nests in trees, buildings and under the ground. They mix plant fibre with saliva to create a paper like substance to build with.

**Think about** ... life inside an animal house.

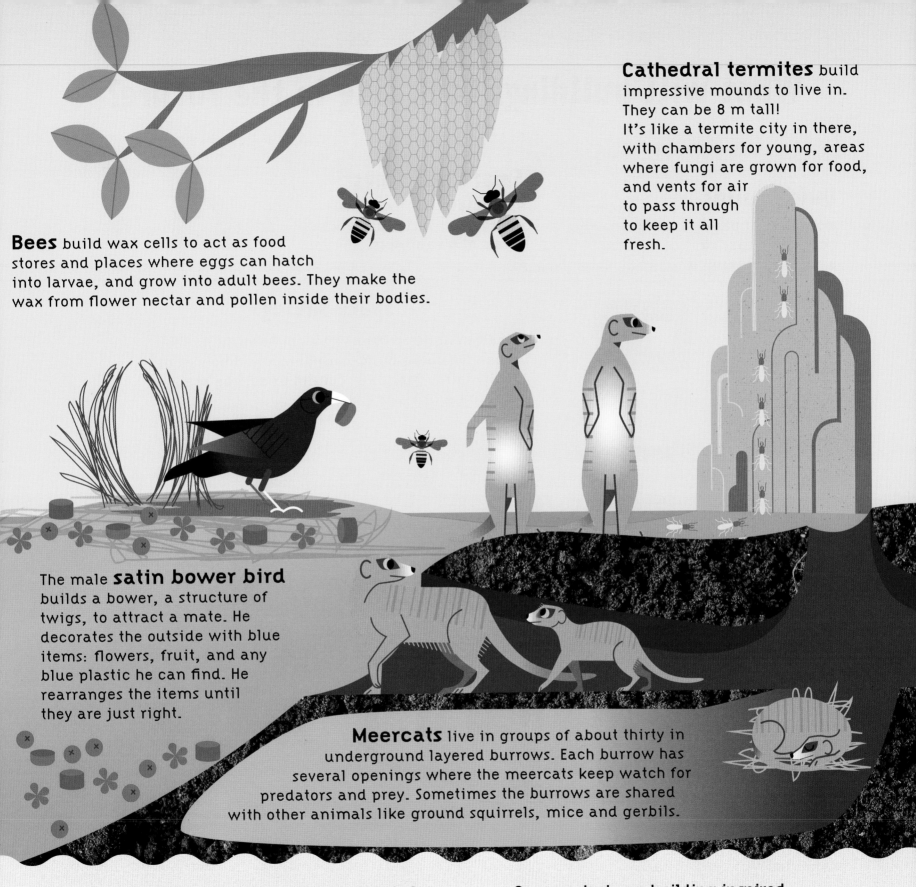

**Cathedral termites** build impressive mounds to live in. They can be 8 m tall! It's like a termite city in there, with chambers for young, areas where fungi are grown for food, and vents for air to pass through to keep it all fresh.

**Bees** build wax cells to act as food stores and places where eggs can hatch into larvae, and grow into adult bees. They make the wax from flower nectar and pollen inside their bodies.

The male **satin bower bird** builds a bower, a structure of twigs, to attract a mate. He decorates the outside with blue items: flowers, fruit, and any blue plastic he can find. He rearranges the items until they are just right.

**Meercats** live in groups of about thirty in underground layered burrows. Each burrow has several openings where the meercats keep watch for predators and prey. Sometimes the burrows are shared with other animals like ground squirrels, mice and gerbils.

Which animal house would you like to live in?
What are the smells, sights and sounds inside?
Can you name any other amazing animal builders?

Can you design a building inspired by an animal home?
What materials would you use?

25

# What will buildings look like in the future?

## Quick builds

Modular flat pack housing is easy to assemble. Houses are constructed from ready-made boxes or panels.

## Smart buildings

Computers will monitor energy and water use and levels of cleanliness.

## Space saving

Electromagnetic lifts mean we could build really tall or long buildings.

We could build more underground houses or build under the sea.

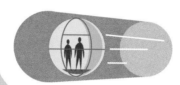

## Linked up

New homes and work places will be joined together by green spaces.

**Think about** ... buildings of the future.

It's estimated that by 2100, people around the world will need to have built about 2 billion more homes to house 11.2 billion people. They will all need buildings to work in, schools and hospitals. Here are some ideas that could help:

## Space

Perhaps there will be buildings in space.

There are plans to build a space hotel that orbits the Earth.

There are lots of plans to build permanent space stations on Mars. Could they be built using ice or Mars dust?

## Sustainable

Use existing empty buildings for living.

Make buildings that are weather, flood and earthquake proof.

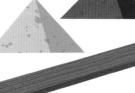

Use readily available materials that are recyclable.

## Robots

Maybe robots could help. Could they use AI technology to design buildings for us?

Use 3D printers to recreate houses and bridges.

Robotic houses could turn to follow light, or shade during the day, making use of natural light and heat sources.

**It's over to you — the future of buildings is in your hands. What buildings can you imagine and design for the future?**

# Many more questions!

1. How did you get into the houses in Çatalhöyük?

2. How were building materials for the Taj Mahal transported?

3. What's the recipe for concrete?

4. How many storeys does the Burj Khalifa have?

5. What is adobe?

6. What's good about living underground?

7. What 3D shapes make up the structure of the Nagoya City Science Museum?

8. What unusual material does Shigeru Ban use for his buildings?

9. What is the Satin Bower Bird's favourite colour?

10. What is glass made from?

# Further information

## Websites

kids.kiddle.co/Building

https://science.howstuffworks.com/engineering-channel.htm

www.sciencekids.co.nz/sciencefacts/engineering/buildings.html

## Books

*Adventures in STEAM: Buildings* by Izzi Howell (Wayland, 2019)

*Awesome Engineering: Skyscrapers* by Sally Spray (Franklin Watts, 2018)

*Wonderwise: Let's Build a House: a book about buildings and materials* by Mick Manning (Franklin Watts, 2014)

# Glossary

**Aerodynamic** – shaped to allow air to pass over smoothly

**AI** (artificial intelligence) – technology designed to make intelligent machines work or think like humans

**Airtight** – sealed, to stop air getting in or escaping

**Amphitheatre** – open-air building with rows of seats surrounding a central area, where entertainment took place

**Archaeologist** – someone who studies ancient people and civilisations by digging up objects or looking at the remains of buildings or structures

**Architect** – someone trained in how to design buildings

**Atrium** – open or glass-roofed entrance or central space in a building

**Burrow** – underground tunnel or hole built by an animal for shelter

**Climate** – the usual weather conditions in an area

**Ellipsoid** – a shape like a squashed sphere

**Energy efficient** – building or object designed to save energy use

**Environmentally friendly** – lifestyle choices, buildings or objects that do less or no harm to the environment

**Fjord** – a deep, narrow inlet on the coast

**Foundations** – solid structures on which a building is built

**Furnace** – a very hot oven, used to melt materials such as metal and glass

**Hearth** – the stone area in a house on which a fire is built

**Insulation** – a material used to cover part of a building or object to keep heat in or out

**Modular** – construction or design using small sections that can be fixed together

**Mortar** – a mixture of sand, water, lime and cement

**Mosaic** – a pattern or picture made from small tiles, stones or glass pieces

**Nomadic** – a way of life involving travelling to different places, sometimes with livestock, in search of fresh grazing

**Pagodas** – a tower with many shaped roofs jutting out from it

**Planetarium** – a dome-shaped building used to educate people about the night sky by projecting images of stars, planets and constellations on the ceiling

**Pyramid** – a large building with a square or triangular base and sloping sides

**Reclaimed** – a previously used material, used in a new way

**Recyclable** – a material or object that can be broken down and made into a new product, such as plastic, glass or paper, or re-used

**Self-sufficient** – able to produce everything you need, without the help of other people

**Settlement** – a place that people gathered to live

**Skyscraper** – a very tall building

**Structure** – something made from different parts

**Sustainable** – using natural materials and energy in such a way that it does not harm the environment

**Tessellated** – a pattern of small flat pieces

**Vent** – an opening that allows air, gas or liquid to pass out or into a building or room

# Game cards

You can play with the game cards in a number of ways:
Choose a buildings card and get a friend to ask questions that you can answer with a yes or no,
e.g. Is it a skyscraper?
They can guess the buildings card through a process of elimination.

**Name** Petronas Towers
**Description**
Twin skyscrapers

**Floor area** 395,000 m²
**Date** 1998
**Cool factor** 9
**Build Bonus** 9

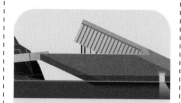

**Name** Under
**Description**
Underwater restaurant

**Floor area** 495 m²
**Date** 2019
**Cool factor** 7
**Build Bonus** 4

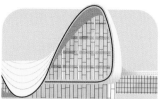

**Name** Heydar Aliyev
Centre
**Description**
Curvy cultural centre

**Floor area** 57,500 m²
**Date** 2007
**Cool factor** 8
**Build Bonus** 8

**Name** The Great Pyramid
of Giza
**Description**
Pointy pyramids

**Floor area** 55,000 m²
**Date** 2560 BCE
**Cool factor** 9
**Build Bonus** 9

**Name** Colosseum
**Description**
Huge
amphitheatre

**Floor area** 24,000 m²
**Date** 80
**Cool factor** 6
**Build Bonus** 7

**Name** Cube Tube
**Description**
Bold Box Building

**Floor area** 13,421 m²
**Date** 2010
**Cool factor** 4
**Build Bonus** 3

**Name** Taj Mahal
**Description**
Marble tomb

**Floor area** 170,000 m²
**Date** 1648
**Cool factor** 10
**Build Bonus** 3

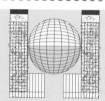

**Name** Nagoya City
Science Museum
**Description**
Sphere between towers

**Floor area** 22,551 m²
**Date** 1962
**Cool factor** 7
**Build Bonus** 4

**Name** Willis Tower
**Description**
Blocky tower block

**Floor area** 416,000 m²
**Date** 1973
**Cool factor** 6
**Build Bonus** 7

**Name** Burj Khalifa
**Description**
Supertall skyscraper

**Floor area** 309,473 m²
**Date** 2010
**Cool factor** 6
**Build Bonus** 10

**Name** Jin Mao Tower
**Description**
Skyscraper

**Floor area** 24,000m²
**Date** 1999
**Cool factor** 8
**Build Bonus** 6

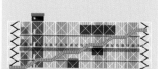

**Name** Centre Pompidou
**Description**
Outside skeleton and
tubes

**Floor area** 100,000 m²
**Date** 1977
**Cool factor** 9
**Build Bonus** 7

**Name** Treehotel
**Description**
Reflecting treehouse

**Floor area** 16 m²
**Date** 2010
**Cool factor** 6
**Build Bonus** 3

**Name** Igloo
**Description**
Cosy ice shelter

**Floor area** 6 m²
**Date** 1200 (est)
**Cool factor** 10
**Build Bonus** 3

**Name** The Ziggurat of Ur
**Description**
Zig-zag stepped tower

**Floor area** 2880 m²
**Date** 2100 BCE
**Cool factor** 6
**Build Bonus** 5

Photograph or scan the cards, print them, cut them out and you can play the following games:

- Top Trumps
- Snap (you will need to print out two sets of cards)
- Lotto (you will need to print out two sets of cards)
- Matching pairs (you will need to print out two sets of cards).

Create your own building cards to add to the pack!

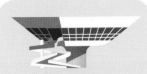

**Name** Niterói Contemporary Art Museum
**Description** Space-age gallery

**Floor area** 400 m²
**Date** 1996
**Cool factor** 8
**Build Bonus** 5

**Name** Shanghai Tower
**Description** Twisting, twirly tower

**Floor area** 80,000 m²
**Date** 2015
**Cool factor** 9
**Build Bonus** 8

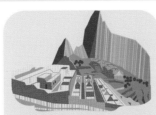

**Name** Machu Picchu
**Description** Ancient Inca city

**Floor area** 32,593 m²
**Date** 1450
**Cool factor** 9
**Build Bonus** 10

**Name** St Basil's Cathedral
**Description** Decorative church

**Floor area** 900 m² (est)
**Date** 1561
**Cool factor** 8
**Build Bonus** 6

**Name** Parthenon
**Description** Cool column temple

**Floor area** 2170 m²
**Date** 432 BCE
**Cool factor** 5
**Build Bonus** 2

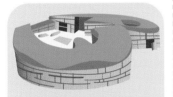

**Name** Skara Brae
**Description** Ancient stone house

**Floor area** 36 m²
**Date** 3000 BCE
**Cool factor** 6
**Build Bonus** 2

**Name** Mars Desert Research Centre
**Description** Space pods on Earth

**Floor area** 111 m²
**Date** 2001
**Cool factor** 5
**Build Bonus** 1

**Name** Shanghai World Financial Centre
**Description** Bottle Opener building

**Floor area** 381,600 m²
**Date** 2008
**Cool factor** 9
**Build Bonus** 7

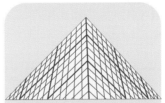

**Name** Louvre Pyramid
**Description** Glossy glass pyramid

**Floor area** 1,000 m²
**Date** 1989
**Cool factor** 4
**Build Bonus** 2

**Name** Sagrada Familia
**Description** Beautiful, bold basilica

**Floor area** 41,000 m²
**Date** Not complete
**Cool factor** 10
**Build Bonus** 2

**Name** Nanchan Temple
**Description** China's oldest timber building

**Floor area** 110 m²
**Date** 782
**Cool factor** 5
**Build Bonus** 1

**Name** Empire State Building
**Description** New York Landmark

**Floor area** 208,879 m²
**Date** 1931
**Cool factor** 8
**Build Bonus** 5

**Name** Through Gardens House
**Description** Modern desert home

**Floor area** 122 m²
**Date** 2017
**Cool factor** 6
**Build Bonus** 3

**Name** Tikal
**Description** Ancient Mayan city

**Floor area** 570,000 m²
**Date** 4 BCE
**Cool factor** 8
**Build Bonus** 8

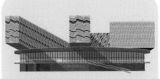

**Name** Moscow School of Management
**Description** Cantilevered cuboids

**Floor area** 42,891 m²
**Date** 2010
**Cool factor** 9
**Build Bonus** 8

# Index